A Bard's View

G. Culshaw

FUTURECYCLE PRESS
www.futurecycle.org

Cover photo by Caroline Lewis; author photo by Caroline Lewis; cover and interior book design by Diane Kistner; Adobe Garamond Pro text and Paddington SC titling

Library of Congress Control Number: 2020932135

Published by FutureCycle Press
Athens, Georgia, USA

ISBN 978-1-942371-84-7

This book is dedicated to Gillian Clarke,
who lit the fireworks within.

CONTENTS

TAKING HER WORDS BACK TO THE SEA

When mum spoke yesterday, I tried
to rewind her to the eighties.
When football matches fell from her
tongue, pints held in her hand, cigarettes
smoked from her mouth.

We ate crisps together on sea walls,
putted golf balls, stood by arcade
machines. Watched roller coasters
glide through the sky as seagulls
bartered for crumbs.

In the social club before the game
under the Old Mold Road End,
I sat on the leather seat of the stool,
the ceiling light dimming my age.
Ashtrays were filled with crumbled fag ends.

I ate crisps with a cinema crunch.
Watched adults come and go.
You brought me here to attach me
to a badge. But all I think about
are the memories that were gone before halftime.

Mother Is Leaving Me

When I went yesterday, I thought
we were in the next life. Mother's body
is being attacked by things I have never
heard of.

I sat on the sofa like I was back
at the train station years ago.
When life was real and we had bellies
full of sandwiches, chips, ice cream,
and doughnuts. When our hair still
grew the color it wished.

Yesterday I looked at her chained
to the calendar. Her bones leaving shells behind
of who she had been. Joints tightening,
nerves numb.

When I got home, I saw the date,
held her face in my palm, kept my tears
inside my skull. Listened to her voice build
a lump in my throat.

I Never Knew My Mother

I never knew my mother
before I was born.
I'm sure she put posters
of sports stars on her wall.

In the photos her hair was black.
I knew she came from the coast,
brought the salt air inland.

There was a factory job
at some point. Her parents
became my grandparents

as I aged. I saw her face
in their features on different
days. Football programs
gave me weekends she'd known.

And under her skin was a rack
of nerves that made me hear her
being told off as a child.

I WATCH FROM MY OWN LIGHTHOUSE

We filled the room with our bodies,
freed the outside from our feet.
Mother lay under the ceiling's light

I listened to their tongues, being
the son and nephew that I am.
There was a time when words spoke

more than body behaviors. When they spoke
to me, a child, and I listened as an owl
perched on a branch.

But today I watch from my own lighthouse,
seeing the crashed waves and storms in the
folded arms, dropped eyes.

They turn silence into loudness.

I Never Knew Him Before

He's never said much to me about before.
The odd night out or horse bet
he won—weeknights watching
the footy.

He mentioned a relationship
ruined by her sister. Times he
watched The Beatles in The Cavern.

I know he planted spuds
in our back garden. Brought home
a wheelbarrow full of horse muck.

He met my mother in the local.
They sang football songs on trains.
I was first, then another followed,

and I started to see who he was.
He never said much about Angela
or if she would ever come back,

but he did say he wanted to see
her again, to ask her why she left.

DAYS OUT ON THE TRAIN

Years ago, train doors had windows
you could pull down, and we
would stick out our calf-heads.

The moving air blew out
science and other school
subjects we hated.

Railway lines bumped along
the wheels, as if juggling
them between each other.

The carriage passed things
we never saw. The day ahead
was already in our minds.

All we had to do was press replay
as the day went by. Bacon
sandwich in a cafe, a can of Coke

from the shop, the press of buttons
on arcade machines. Laughter and spit
and us—carrying a strut from our place of birth.

HIDE AND SEEK

When the fog came out at night,
we would treat it like daytime.
Hoodies up, hats on, gloves
inflated with hands.

Hide and seek, as we counted
under a streetlight. Your turn
to find us as we'd melt into the dark.
Knee bends behind cars, hedges,

garden gates. Lying flat on the tarmac,
we listened to the underworld.
Held our lungs until they popped,
then we let out slug-speed air.

The fog had no clock to listen
for. We ran into it, unaware
of what might happen or where we'd go,
whether it was the next day or sleep

from the night before.

Bike Rides At Night

When the world was flat, we travelled
on mountain bikes. Read street signs
as we pedaled towards leaving school.

Our bikes gave us distance, took us
away from living rooms that hemmed
in our words. Gears were clicking

on every hill. At night streetlights
shimmied on. Brought V-shaped
patterns of light to slow pavements down.

Car headlights made us think.
Zebra crossings made us jump.
Pub doorways quickened our feet.

When we got home, our legs burned
away homework. Our minds bottled
up the bike rides, turned them to chutney

so we could use them years later
on salads when we were bored in adulthood.

A STREET WE PLAYED IN

There was a street we played in.
We ran up and down to wake it up.
Neighbors looked through netting,
watched our bones grow as trees.

The ball bounced into gardens.
We tapped latches, pushed wooden
frames, jumped locked gates.
Ran away from snappy dogs,

ignored shouting grandmothers,
hid from frowning granddads.
We nodded to friends, parents. We ate
bananas in summer, pot noodles

in winter. Our tongues filled our
mouths, licked the sky, shouted
words that fell into neighbors'
chimney pots. Sometimes in autumn

we would collect conkers, keep
them in our pockets to help us grow.

THE ICE CREAM VAN DAYS

When the ice cream van came,
we ran out of the house in shorts.
Its engine throbbed, woke up
the street. We held small coins,

passed them to the man through
a gap in his van. He leaned out
to check prices with his hair balancing
on his skull. Cones stood upside down,

reached for the ceiling. Parents smoked
in the queue. A slosh machine
churned colors school hadn't shown us.
Our hands eager to hold, our tongues

longed to lick. Lips rubbed against
each other. Neighbors used their
mouths to talk. We sat on walls
with frozen gums, felt a part of something,

smiled at people twice our age.

A DAY OUT

We went there in our teenage
car—unfurled school years
on the motorway.

The sea stayed with us
as we made our way
to the coast.

Arcade machines, fairground
rides took the voices that
sprang from pre-adult throats.

Wallets we had as Christmas
presents emptied loose talk.

We took in the salty air,
brought it home with us,
then slept under the stars,

heard our footprints in the sand
being washed away.

An Old Friend

I was thinking of him the other day
when we played snooker or tennis,
kicked a football around, and swigged
pints until our eyes glazed.

Your black hair stung white clouds,
the athletic body hidden under your
clothes. Those days back in school,
you were the big drinker, drew your name

on all our tongues. When we left,
things changed. Clubbing stretched
out your weekends into the early hours
of weekdays. I'd become hemmed

within my skull. You hadn't.
Years later I caught up, but you
had already turned back to who
you were. So we left each other's

voices on the roads we walked.
Maybe one day they will be heard again.

An Old Childhood Friend

He was the first person to show me
goalkeeper gloves. Held football
chants in his gut. He had left secondary
school by the time I got there. Then

he started smoking and going to the pub,
things I thought only my parents did.
He spray-painted a football goal
on a brick wall, had a laugh that livened

up summer. Friends followed
him to our patch: Dilly Hodges, Gary
Grot, Bodman, and others who spoke
a language we were yet to grow.

We played football until the sun
fell away, sat on curbs with cramps
in our bums. He once told me I
was his best friend.

I wonder what he is doing now
that he lives on another planet.

MEMORIAL DAYS

We had come out of the teenage
tunnel, saw new light up ahead.
Our bodies, minds, changing.

Bent forward, elbows tight, feet
firm with eyeballs solid as glass.
Acute or obtuse angles calculated.

Striking one to nudge another,
blast or tap. Sometimes a shave shot
to roll for the fish-catch pocket.

Numbers added up on the board.
It was a voyage allowing us to view
the table of what lay ahead.

We did our best to work things
through, but snooker is a long game
with angles becoming more acute with time.

A DOOR INTO THE DARK

A naked bulb hung, a hidden light
until you flicked the switch.
Then cobwebs shone, bristled frost.

Rust tried to shy away from its moss-like
spread. Tools deep in retirement
blinked in the sunlight.

I had stirred him from hibernation.
We pulled out handles with metal heads,
opened box lids like a doctor's brief.

Swept away crawling memories,
gave his hands a purpose. The old grip
twist, finger pinch, thumb press,
came back, back from the dark.

THE DYING FARM

Like shuffling feet that edge
towards train doors, their heads
jostle for the trough full of rain,

Tassel tails flap as breeze-
blown windsocks, the grass
forgotten under hoof-trodden land.

A round-neck jumper armors
a man who has stuffed a thousand
years under his fingernails.

A cottage sits like a corpse's skull.
Barns take in the wind, allowing
it to leave at will.

The sun never alights here,
always stops short. A heap
of used tires, now blanked out.

LENTHAL STREET

The bypass went through my ears.
Engines shattered the mind.
Doors, windows ran like snake scales.
Pavements cracked from heavy syllables.

Two steps up to a wooden door, opened
to a fallow rug. She shuffled as if keeping
things from growing,
dragged her life with each pull of limb.

Water boiled in a pan, the lid nervous.
I wrote my name in the net of glass
that caught her breath. Dust, skin
shredded in the turn of time.

She held the ticking bread, sawing it with
a weakening arm, slices unevenly cut,
crumbs strewn as first snow.
Then I heard my name fade into her history
as her voice called me for dinner.

SHOES

He would walk more miles in a day than
anybody else in town. Each step seemed
a hindrance to where he wanted to be.

Kicking up road dust and dead skin, his soles
would rub down, leave a trail of rubber.
Two, three, four times a day he would go out,
as if something sinking made him move;

"Thumbs up" to beeping cars,
fist clenched when the "Blues" won.
For every pair he made in Dunlop,
he wore away in life.

But now his shadow has caught up.
He sits for hours, restless, fidgety,
as if his feet are walking all over his skin.

A WELDED JOINT

I slipped on the sunlight.
My arm creaked as boat decking,
Siberian tiles shivered my childhood.

Straightaway he picked me up,
drove me to hospital. Our hands
knitted together on that journey.

Though I do not remember the plaster,
he helped mend the joint.
With his adjustable hands,

he welded my tears, rubbed life
into my skin. Later on, father
watched, out of touch, out of joint.

ANGEL WING

It was her birthday, and we went for a drive
ending up in a jaunt around the Mere.
Time was as flat and slow as the lake.

There were park benches lined up like mattresses
for the drunkards. Left-behind cigarette stubs
for the down-and-outs that needed some baccy.

A staggering walker came over, his body
leaning to one side. I looked on, weary, ready
to protect. He looked at me, his eyes begging

"Pass me some! Pass me some!"

I was a dealer to him, a doctor, a medicine man.
He was a goose who had lost his way.
Now drugged to the eyeballs on flour and water,
he stared at me.

A goose beater, a goose bully, a food stealer,
his life a misery addicted to white powder.

I looked at him and shook my head. I am a part
of the society that has made him deformed.
And I felt guilty all the way to the car.

Yesterday

I stroked the heavy paint across the concrete sill.
Spider webs in triangle shapes sat in corners.
The sun bounced off the glass, showed me the world
behind.

Black paint glimmered like fresh tarmac.
I pushed the web-strands into air holes
and wear-and-tear knocks.

I was him, painting the steps, sills, gates,
outside pipework. Every other year "Mind the Step"
or "Wet Paint" on paper lay as hints on a floor.

He would even do the neighbors with his helpful
attitude. I was never asked to help or shown how,
but as I have aged a fermenting has taken place.

Now I check verticals and horizontals as I balance
my own life, my own home, for the years to come.

PASSING TREES

I see old friends like passing trees,
their lives spreading maps and rings.

One, for all his strength, stare and growl,
was struck by a storm that brought him down.

Some sprouted branches like a sea anemone
gasping for air, gasping to be seen.

Another has left behind a skeleton of himself,
having been and gone, life too short.

I see old friends today as I pass by and by.

TUNES

Next to the cattle market,
a long alleyway room where electric-
looking chairs waited. Tunes the barbers.

"Right to the bone," he would order. I sat
quietly as the snipping teeth bumped along.

Tractor-chugging graders ran through
in bends over the hill-shaped heads.

The cow dung wafted in, sometimes
filling our nostrils with farm life.

I was always glad to get out, well mowed.
Groaning came from next door as we left.

My father took us there.
He was a city boy, so it was new to us both.

Flatcap men, dull-colored clothes,
hoof kicking, stomping cattle.

Prisoners tinned, squeezed into trailers,
took to new hills, all waiting to be cut.

TRANSMITTING

He would sit in the kitchen,
Mother and me in the living room.
The wall prevented things, slight
reception through an open door.

You would have to listen to hear.
As he gave us statements that lingered,
he was on a different wavelength to us both.
A crackling fuzz sometimes echoed.

He was somewhere we could not see.
Tuning in with him was tough.
Only now, as his voice has weakened,
does he listen. The once-strong wind

that came from afar is now a zephyr
whispering slowly away, slowly away.

Shadows of Tryfan

Once there was life upon you,
growing up, growing strong.

Until you came to a stop, setting
out your figure amongst the rest.

Today your shadow weakens
as you erode back to the earth.

As a child, I came to you for support
to build my cartilage and bone.

Your rock face in the morning light,
deep in slumber, ravaged by weather.

For years we have walked all over you,
pushed you deeper, further away.

One day you will be gone;
then we will walk in silence, grieving.

BUTEO BUTEO

You can walk past one if quiet enough
and even then it will only be a hang-glider
throw out of a tree. The walnut-brown wings

stretch out into the air. There's no urgency
in its flow, a rough sort of flier harassed
by corvids, misunderstood by gamekeepers

and such like. It is library-gentle all day, just
pottering about, wearing its baggy trousers, running
like a chicken after scurrying creatures.

Conker-feathered, herring-silver under each wing,
this bird is not a swimmer of the sky but more
a heavy wagon plod. Occasionally some will

go to the clouds, circling and nasal-shouting at the land
before perching as a neighbor in a block
of flats, watching the passing people go by down below.

THE BLACKBIRD OF US

In the lifeless back garden, I once knew
your cold, distant song was plaguing the senses.
I would hear your eighteen-beat life.

Not a week went by without you there.
I'm sure Father knew; Mother, maybe not.
Your song would come in spurts, skittish verse,

short-lived, that left us aching more.
But your black feathers told me you were gone.
Eighteen months, eighteen beats, eighteen beats—

repeating over and over until the lid shut tight.
Then off you flew, leaving the deadweight silence
of passed flight that still echoes in the hedgerow.

WHIXALL MOSS

We would be carried there in a bumpy
van: bends, bends, and more bends.
No straight roads to keep things simple.

A vacant land, ghostly fog, last breath
of the bog cutters. Flat cap, elbows tired,
palm worn, back tethered.

Adders lingered in the alleyway tufts;
owl echoes plopped in squelchy puddles.
Spongy clumps, unstable steps, made us
wary of a fall. The bog could suck you up,

keep you preserved for a thousand years,
pickled in your own sweat.
We have drained enough of her land,

taken away the blood of her own body.
Now we start to give it back, though she will say

"I never gave it to you anyway."

Autumn Wood Eats Things You Know

It takes the daylight, sends it to the stars
above. It eats birds; coughed-up feathers
lie on the edge of things,

regurgitated meals. Clean white bones
lie like spare car parts. Snowdrops come
and go. A pool of bluebells is slowly drunk.

Daffodils fade to green stems. Stand
alone, lost-looking. Their yellow lives
nibbled for weeks by something unseen.

Cow parsley is enticed to grow, to cloud
before a slow breath whispers it away,
leaving unripe-looking scaffold frames.

The wood eats things you know.
Best not to linger there too long
or you may be taken, too.

Spirit of the Wood

I see her in the tree ahead, a foreign
body to the wood and bark.

Mottled feathers, snow and mud,
a used path two days after a snowfall.

She is receiving the night
that bounces, trots and calls;

she is receiving the night's
squeaking, sniffling, whining, yawns.

She is the night's gunshot, the keeper
of the world: anyone steps out of line,

down she swoops.

The wings are oars rowing the darkness,
sweeping away the light from the withering sun.

Her slingshot tongue is a rock-splintering tone
that spears the pitch-black where stars fall in.

OLD BARN

I pass this place every day to work.
The slipped slates show naked beams.

Wind brushing shavings off the stone walls
eventually leaves a skeleton building,
a knot on the bark of the landscape.

Pigeons might come to have a look
before they coo with their bingo-hall natter.

The earth is taking back what is hers. Wood,
sedimentary rock, metamorphic rock, metal
as shaped brackets, hinges and bolts.

All being swallowed into the mouth
of the thing we call home—the very stomach
slowly digesting the lot of us.

THE ALLEYWAY OF TWO GATES

When his wife went into a home,
I came to see him as much as I could.
Two gates sat opposite in the alleyway;
one led to him, the other led to sorrow.

Using the one gate became an everyday thing.
Page-turning it for shopping trips, hanging
washing, taking his weekly rubbish to the bin.

He missed using the opposite gate;
hinges weeped, squeaked its joints,
showed the afterlife of retirement.

I did my best to help open it, give him the life
he missed, resuscitate his working hands.
His eyes opened when we went through.

But when we came back, the lonely butter knife,
rumbling washer, fairy bubbles in the sink,
days-old bread, and stacked-up clothes showed
the split in the alleyway that was his heart.

STEREOTYPE

He looked like one of them, you know?
Red-cheeked as if left outside all night;
paper-thin skin showed blood vessels.

Whiskey breath on a morning drive to work;
standing in the local, nod here, nod there.

The prejudiced frowns, anger towards
the government. Sometimes he had the look
of a man straining on the loo.

He's one of them, you know? Carry on till he drops
like a ship when the world was flat. Brought
up in the same way as his father who smoked

and drank, probably had a tattoo somewhere.
They shared a fag at the back door while Mother
sliced potatoes into chips for the fryer.

HE HAS LEFT HIS COAT BEHIND

The fox has left his coat behind
as it lies on the floor, boneless.
The wood has pulled him out
of it like a foot out of a sock.

He is somewhere else now,
naked and questioning.
Wandering alone, his shadow
has melted into the night,

adding more darkness
to the already heavy sky
that we have created.

EMPTY HEADED

The box that sits on his neck
is the coffin of his father.
His eyes have not woken
since that last turn of a spade.

He is vacant of the world
as a hand in a glove.
He walks the shop aisles
as if in a procession.

The different voices that come
from his grave-gut sometimes
make you wonder if he knows
what he is saying.

When will the door open
to allow him to leave? I do not know.
But we are all dead to him
like cattle awaiting the hook.

BUTCHERS

The last shop before a run of houses:
Jones the butchers, father to son, father to son,
passed down or up depending on your outlook.

String-wrapped slabs like parcels, felt-tip
markings on white labels—ounces, grams,
pounds, kilos—things I never knew the weight of.

Ruby red, creamy red, blood red, brick red;
shoelace mince, sand-colored pies.
Brown paper bags swung by finger and thumb,
the firm press and hold of a butcher's hand.

But today it is gone, the meat dried out,
shop awning flickering in the wind. I hear my
footsteps walking along the pavement as we pass
in the car.

SEEING THINGS

I went with him once, sitting
at the pond side. He loved the

reel of things, casting hope into
the unknown, breaking the skin

of silence. His float would "plop."
Plop! Plop! Plop! A light hand

for such an age, as if he already
knew the best way to live. Mine

was a "dunk" cracking the pond
like ice water, not thinking

of what might be next. Haven't
seen him for years. Maybe he still
goes. Searching for the unknown,

breaking the stillness with a light
touch. As I mature such a thing.

A Surge of Life

Like a full moon, he only
comes now and again.
But when he does, a new
sky follows.

An electrician by trade, his flick
of light changes what we see.
Many switches clicked,
wires pulled to a live source;

he gives energy to dead bricks
and allows machines to have a reason.
When he visits us, a fresh surge
goes through the house,

gives us all a buzz,
adding fresh batteries to our
fading voices before he vaults
back over the border to home.

Rucksack

There's a sketch on square paper,

ruler and pencil surgically lying.

Fabric cut with light fingers.

Two straps and a rucksack-shaped

bay. Not complete, with Velcro

and sewing still to be done.

You are preparing to move into adulthood,

chauffeuring your own world, emotion.

Taking the load that has grown.

Years from now we will wonder

what you have inside, hoping you

may let us see, so we can help.

POTTING SHED

In there somewhere, a dice-shake of a pot,
as if leveling out the unsettled,
before placing a broad bean
of button weight into the compost.

Canes lazily stood, like children in a PE
lesson, in the flatcap thickness of a grow bag.
Then things would be belted up by string
for the sun-growth of a tomato plant.

In open egg boxes sat seed potatoes
shaped like tie-knots, each waiting to burst
tendrils into the air like a newborn octopus.

This was his greenhouse, his extension to the land.

ON PASSING A FARM WHILE ON A TRAIN

Rusting harrow lying still.

Overused pallets, broken slats.

Tires, tires, tires, tires, tires.

Two wandering crows.

A stack of old bricks webbed and mossed.

Lichen crawling yearly along the fence rail.

A boot flung away.

Unused chicken wire, still rolled tight.

"Not got round to."

Hernia hill ready to pop.

Arthritis just waiting around the corner.

Two tractors, one in use, the other not.

Jobs building up:

Barbed wire hanging, logs need chopping.

Wheelbarrow full. Farmer's grip loosening.

Leave it till the next life. Leave it for now.

MIXING THINGS UP

We would stand there waiting, hoping,
our grip on a wooden handle, T-shaped,
with the other hand on the mid-life,

ready to lift something weighty
off the mind—not that we knew it back
then. A mix of sand, water, cement.

Tumbling along, moaning, groaning,
as you tilted the shovel plate, hearing
a sloppy sigh of release from the turn of things.

Ticking by with every mouth-load, knead
the mix, then wait for the chance
to bond, build from what it gave you.

Before a shoulder lift and fill,
grip the handle, raise the hope along
with every bump of the one-tire wheelbarrow.

SNOOKER SOUNDTRACK

Memorial Hall,
usually our days off.

The gathering of the reds,
rolling pebbles on a beach.

Chalking the cue tip,
sand rubbing between toes.

Pint glass plonked on the table,
the window closed on a train.

Mutterings from lung-smoked men,
a beehive in a bush.

The ball dropping into a netted pocket,
fish caught out at sea.

HAZEL STICK

The thump of his hazel stick
where he waits and slowly breathes.
His running collie with a hunter's nose.

Mountains still, sleeping rough,
their greenery backs silver-cold.
His gentle feet tap the hill.

Vast valleys of sweet river air.
Lungs relaxed, calm his oak bone.

Collie is bouncing, bounding, rounding up,
a four-legged lasso. He walks
the mountains of his mind, smooths out

the problems he has faced. How I long
for the thump of his hazel stick.

JOHAN CRUYFF

He ran along with confidence;
studs on his boots tickled the soil
lightly as a child's hand-tapped wood.

He took the watcher away from mud
and stud and plumes of cigarette smoke
that discolored the sky.

His moves planned, five passes ahead.
Knew the diagonals of the pitch. He gently
brushed the pitch as if it was thin ice.

When he touched the ball, it sounded
like a putter on the green. His feet moved
as two disturbed fish at a river's edge.

He gave the corner flags a reason and painted
the pitch as he passed the ball. People chased
after him, but even today we're still far behind.

COLLEGE

The tap of a stretcher against another, buttering up the Flemish bond. Things laid out before me, a building up of maturity. The wall of knowledge that leads us through life.

A slide and heave of trowel under sloppy mortar: tilt and pull back, leaving a slug-like trail. The bed to rest a brick, the tip-tap of a handle. A knock-knock on an empty house door.

I built what I could before I left, not knowing the future but knowing what you build in life should have support. The lintel became too heavy, and eventually I had to carry my own load.

When I see empty buildings and old warehouses with windows sad-looking and broken, I know I made the right choice to let bricks sit under their own guilt, their own weight.

CHOMOLUNGMA

In the Rongbuk glacier, a shoal of tents
is stranded as if washed up by a forgotten sea.
Sherpas, gap-toothed, conker brown with
calluses that stretch across their palms
like the Himalayas themselves.

A heave and a squat, grimace and sweat.
Carrying other people's loads. The clanking
of pots could be mistaken for rattling bones.
But what do people care when their boots
are sent back to the homes, sitting like a pair

of lungs on their porch.

CAMPING WITH A YOUTH WORKER

The moon was a sliced apple
sky—a used matchstick black.
We sat under flickering cats' eyes
telling stories we could not yet hear.

Me, Paxo and Rob sat in the vastness
of the open country. A world without walls
or doors. Thought we would be friends forever.

The field was soggy with a seeping lake;
bucket-deep puddles randomly placed.
We shook with heavy laughter.
The barriers to home life were taken down.

We felt freedom. Our shallow breaths
travelled far and wide.
Thought we would be friends forever, forever.

ANEMONE

There comes a time when what you have
has to be protected like the petals
of an anemone, folding together at night,
protect the heart from cold and frost

tThen open out for the delights
of the sun's rays of light.
I do the same with you when you come
home from work. But only in my heart

because I know that, if you knew,
then life would eventually have a say.
So I keep things quiet, fold my arms
around you at night when you dream.

GARDENING HIS FUTURE

For years he had worked with us.
Then it was a van, tools, a loan;
a wheelbarrow carted his old life.

Spades waited like oven peels
longing to palm away some earth.
He snipped roses, lopped branches,

shoveled dirt, edged lawns
as he ploughed a garden in his mind.
The rake that pulled in the sun

scraped away the leaves,
scratched green blades of litter.
The past composted, leaving

behind the sweat of a logo,
his hands free, released
from the knot of a tie.

CONKERS

For some reason, he is picking
up conkers again. Places them
in a tub in the kitchen.

He is squirreling, as his childhood
serves his adulthood. Stretches out
from the top of two decades of life.

Passport ready to be stamped,
brochures with eye-licking photos.
Thumbing brown shells that are

Nature's safes, looking for the code
to open up new growth, add a ring.
They sit like jewels, clean, shiny,

rubbed as a cricket ball upon the leg,
waiting to explode new shoots,
spread new roots for him to follow.

I myself pick up a few.

LINES

We marked the pitch with coats and bags
for goalposts, the only distance on the field
that mattered, like a horizon line to an outgoing

ship. Football is about lines, but only inch lengths.
A pass has to roll to the foot, not bounce.
A corner has to land on the head, not attack

like a cannonball. In adulthood, the lines
become curved as you realize the meaning
of experience. When we were kids, straight lines

were all that mattered and the game was kick
and rush: heavy breathing, tired legs, flicks
of sweat off the brow, a passing of time that always

went quick.

MORTAR MAN

I always remembered him as the mortar man.
On occasion, he would come out, puff a ciggie.
The big wheel turned sand, lime until it became
a cake mix; water would fill from a hose,
splashing us in the eyes, which we would rub
and rub until a burn built up, an itchy burn.

He would sit there on his sofa, a sandy sofa.
One you could pat and see haze fill the room.
A *Daily Mirror* rolled up, a coffee-stained mug,
bricks in a corner—broken bricks, that is.
They would be thrown into the mixer to clean
any scum and crust that built up.

We would press dried mortar between our fingers,
feel the grainy bits as if our bones were fading
away. Push the wheelbarrow in coffin-
heavy steel toecaps. The mortar man would
watch us, puff a rollie, watch the seagulls
fly over, then walk away.

THE GULL

Tomorrow does not exist for me.
I'm a wanderer of the above,
a cloud-surfer, a wind passenger.

I see the grey below, chase the smells.
I believe I can fly forever
between landfill and amenity.

Pecking at disposed lavish all day long,
snapping at moldy bread, scrimping meat
before wolfing fly-blown bin waste.

The journey there and back is only
a mile, same lines, same paths.
You have made me and keep me going.

When my instincts have told me enough
is enough, my stomach will try
to melt down plastic.

I will shit polystyrene, create snow
from my behind. I'll blame you
for that as you made me like this.

SWALLOWS

They pencil the fields in grids,
the white chests and dabs of red.

Their flight is curved, a bobsleigh track
hidden in the air. A turn and sprint then
swoop.

Just above the wheat, snatching
at gnats and other flying things.
I loved it. The occasional beep beep

slightly muffled out my way-sound
with their banana-shaped wings
and bottle opener forms,

moving my eyeballs in directions
they had not gone since learning
double-joined writing in junior school.

Barn Owl

Her feathers are snow collected in a vase
with eyes awake in a sleeping world.

Her satellite head moves like an opened
parachute that's pulled by a running man.

The branch holds no weight, and the tree
stands like a pen in an ink pot.

But then there's a take-off. Her talons titter,
then wake like a thief's hand in a shop.

Swooping down, her wings brush the darkness
as gently as frost on blades of grass.

Her feet grape-crush when landing on the sack
of fur, squeezing her life weight,

before the tail stiffens for the next life.

ROOKS

They have been in the fields all day,
walking like judges in a courtroom,
their susurration teasing the earth.

Black feathers glint as if a star is caught.
They peck at the ground, pickaxe worms,
wood lice. A turned-over field is heaven

for such a humble-looking rabble.
But here they strike into the feeble,
caw-like trapped animals in a cage.

Stabbing, pecking, the black swads
give a subfusc manner to the terrain,
turn it into a savannah.

They wait to strike any passing buzzard,
show them who are the kings of the farm fields.

The Tenor

You are a scatterer of a song, a fire alarm
when I come to the lawn. You whistle
gently in the morning, unzipping the light

from the coming horizon. A grazer of grass
in the hop hop hop of things. After the rain
the wetness gives your feathers a shine.

A nacket is a beetle or woodlouse. A worm
is a meal and peppered seed a nibble. I watch
you ploutering in the puddles on the lane.

Before a prankle in the sunlight to show
your wife. Then off to a hedgerow where you
tenor the garden with delight and purpose.

THE SCREECHING

The mist is thick, solid-looking
as if the whole world has created
a wall around me. I can see no more,

hear nothing, nor taste nor smell the eroding
earth beneath my feet. I am dead
but want to be alive. The earth has gone!

I must be a ghost in a dream.
But then the field cracks in two and, torn
apart as a mouth, sends out a scream.

The fox screeches into the mist, wakes me
up. I am alive again. But the scream
echoes into my heart, scythes my skin.

I jump, scared, shocked! I'm cut into by
the teeth of the dog fox. With every kill,
he has digested their pain and sends it out

into the night sky. I am dead as I walk
back into the house, shaking underneath.
I am a rabbit in the mouth being eaten alive.

BEFORE ME

I was not expecting it as I headed
up the lane for home, but before me
two fritillaries danced midair like
two children dabbing painted hands
on a sheet of paper.

It was that sort of movement,
and I stood before it while our stone
cottage loomed before us in the distance.

But here I was, suspended in time;
then off they went, a chase, an escape
into and beyond the nettles.

RACECOURSE GROUND

The floodlights were a height unknown
to my eyes. Tilting my head back, gazing
at the shining sky. The dew wet

on the grass, players kicked a heavy ball.
A weighty thud seemed to shake the pitch
with every bounce. Ball boys mingled; stewards

in fluorescent coats talked, smoked, blew clouds.
I never knew back then that today I would miss
those days and nights. Being with you both, following,

listening to your footy talk, catching players' names
before the smell of hot dogs floated into my nose.
We would walk around the ground, taking it in,

programs in hand, scarf-wrapped, the world
just a pitch of lines and light and the three of us.

LLANDANWG

Wet dreadlocks of seaweed
lie over muted rocks. They wait
for the water so they can wave
like octopus legs.

We are snapping points in time
as we walk along, balancing on shoulder-
worn pebbles. The earth is moving,
shrugs the sea as an itch.

I watch a wave vomit white
spider legs that crawl over the silence.
We carry on, hopscotch a rock,
stretch a limb, swivel a foot.

Doing our best to ignore
the very thing that soaks our feet.

Merthyr Farm

Some gates closed, others open,
like unfinished books agape.
Fence posts standing
pointless, wandering.

A wind blows wire barriers that
tilt back and fro through
the seasons. A digger bucket sits
like false teeth in a bathroom.

Stone walls hold the fields
together. You sense if they
fell, the sward would avalanche
away as sheets of ice.

THE PHONE RANG

While I waited on the other side,
my ear tensed with every buzz.
Then a life entered; her breath
came in like the tide.

And I thought I was a child
with a seashell again.
Her words came to me slowly,
then each word caught the other up

as her wave gathered strength.
Then she went to look for Caroline
with the ticking clock sound
from every tap of her walking stick.

And I hear the time tap away.

ACKNOWLEDGMENTS

Grateful acknowledgment to the following publications in which these poems first appeared, some in slightly different versions:

Allegro: "Yesterday"
Amaryllis: "Passing Trees," "Coffin Headed"
Basil O'Flaherty: "Lines"
The Cape Rock: "He's Left His Coat Behind"
Dawntreader: "Before Me"
Dimeshow: "Memorial Days"
The Journal: "Camping with a Youth Worker"
Limestone: "Buteo Buteo"
London Grip: "The Dying Farm"
Magma: "Snooker"
The New Ulster: "The Gull"
Panoplyzine: "Mixing Things Up"
Poetry Quarterly: "Chomolungma"
Poppy Road: "Autumn Wood Eats Things You Know"
The Quail Bell: "Seeing Things"
Sentinel: "Mortar Man"
Third Wednesday: The Old Barn"
Virtual Verse: "Angel Wing," "Transmitting"
Whispers: "Gardening His Own Future"
Whixall Moss: "Obsessed with Pipework"

I would like to thank Ty Newydd for allowing me to visit and find my love for poetry. Thanks to Maura Dooley, an exceptional human and wonderful poet. Love and appreciation for friendship and advice to Lynne Caddick, Helen Kay, Pat Edwards, Carolyne Martin, Audrey Adern Jones, David Chorlton, Alice Harrison, and all at Shrewsbury Stanza Group. Thanks also to poetry friends from Ty Newydd and Manchester Met University. And, last but not least, a hero of life, Mr. Jasper.

ABOUT FUTURECYCLE PRESS

FutureCycle Press is dedicated to publishing lasting English-language poetry books, chapbooks, and anthologies in both print-on-demand and Kindle ebook formats. Founded in 2007 by independent editor/publishers and partners Diane Kistner and Robert S. King, the press incorporated as a nonprofit in 2012. A number of our editors are distinguished poets and writers in their own right, and we have been actively involved in the small press movement going back to the early seventies.

The FutureCycle Poetry Book Prize and honorarium is awarded annually for the best full-length volume of poetry we publish in a calendar year. Introduced in 2013, our Good Works projects are anthologies devoted to issues of universal significance, with all proceeds donated to a related worthy cause. Our Selected Poems series highlights contemporary poets with a substantial body of work to their credit; with this series we strive to resurrect work that has had limited distribution and is now out of print.

We are dedicated to giving all of the authors we publish the care their work deserves, making our catalog of titles the most diverse and distinguished it can be, and paying forward any earnings to fund more great books.

We've learned a few things about independent publishing over the years. We've also evolved a unique, resilient publishing model that allows us to focus mainly on vetting and preserving for posterity poetry collections of exceptional quality without becoming overwhelmed with bookkeeping and mailing, fundraising activities, or taxing editorial and production "bubbles." To find out more, come see us at www.futurecycle.org.

THE FUTURECYCLE POETRY BOOK PRIZE

All full-length volumes of poetry published by FutureCycle Press in a given calendar year are considered for the annual FutureCycle Poetry Book Prize. This allows us to consider each submission on its own merits, outside of the context of a contest. Too, the judges see the finished book, which will have benefitted from the beautiful book design and strong editorial gloss we are famous for.

The book ranked the best in judging is announced as the prize-winner in the subsequent year. There is no fixed monetary award; instead, the winning poet receives an honorarium of 20% of the total net royalties from all poetry books and chapbooks the press sold online in the year the winning book was published. The winner is also accorded the honor of being on the panel of judges for the next year's competition; all judges receive copies of all contending books to keep for their personal library.

www.ingramcontent.com/pod-product-compliance
Lightning Source LLC
Chambersburg PA
CBHW070011100426
42741CB00012B/3198